Genocide

R. G. Grant

PRODUCED IN ASSOCIATION WITH
AMNESTY INTERNATIONAL

AMNESTY
INTERNATIONAL
UNITED KINGDOM

WAYLAND

Talking Points series
Alcohol
Animal Rights
Charities – Do They Work?
Divorce
Genocide
Homelessness
Mental Illness
Slavery Today

Editor: Jason Hook
Series editor: Alex Woolf
Designer: Simon Borrough
Consultant: Amnesty International

First published in 1998 by
Wayland Publishers Ltd, 61 Western Road,
Hove, East Sussex, BN3 1JD, England.

Find Wayland on the Internet at
http://www.wayland.co.uk

**British Library Cataloguing in
Publication Data**
Grant, Reg
  Genocide. - (Talking points)
  1.Genocide - Juvenile literature
  1.Title
  364.1'51

ISBN 0 7502 2181 X

Printed and bound in Italy by G.Canale &
C.S.p.A., Turin

**This title produced in association with
Amnesty International UK.**
Amnesty International is a worldwide human
rights movement which is independent of any
government, political faction, ideology,
economic interest or religious creed.
(See page 63.)

**The views expressed in this publication
do not necessarily reflect the views of
Amnesty International.**
Note that Amnesty International only ever uses
the word genocide in its specific legal sense
(see page 5) rather than in the wider sense
employed in this book.

Picture acknowledgements
Amnesty International 52 (Stephen Dupont);
Ancient Art & Architecture 10; AFP 33, 50;
Associated Press AP 7, 38; Camera Press 8, 11
(Jennifer Beeston), 12, 15 (Steve Cox), 23
(Robbie King), 25 (Russell Johnson, top), 25
(bottom), 26 (Ranko Cukovic), 27 (Ivan
Meacci), 28 (Benoit Gysembergh), 32
(Yevegnny Khaldei), 34 (ABC Ajansi), 41
(Benoit Gysembergh), 54 (Steve Cox), 55
(Jacques Haillot, top), (B. Rafaeli, bottom);
Chris Schwartz 4, 9 (bottom), 59; David King
18, 19; Frank Spooner 36; Hulton Getty 9
(top), 17, 24, 30, 31, 46, 49; Panos 5 (Betty
Press), 53 (Betty Press), 57 (Eric Miller);
Popperfoto 22, 47; Popperfoto/Reuters 6, 16,
29, 35, 37, 40, 43, 44, 48, 51, 56, 58; Robert
Harding 45; Topham 13, 14, 21 (Associated
Press), 39.

Contents

What is genocide?

Throughout history, humans have massacred, tortured and enslaved other humans. But only in the twentieth century have people felt the need for a term to describe the annihilation of entire peoples.

The word 'genocide' was invented in 1944, during the Second World War. At this time, the forces of Nazi Germany, led by the dictator Adolf Hitler, were systematically massacring millions of people in the areas of Europe the Nazis occupied. The Nazis had set up death camps to carry out this extermination.

The ruins of Auschwitz-Birkenau, a camp in which the Nazis killed about a million people.

Legal expert Raphael Lemkin invented the word by combining the ancient Greek word *genos*, meaning a race or tribe, and the Latin *cide*, which means killing. Lemkin defined genocide as 'the destruction of a nation or of an ethnic group'. He used the word to describe what the Nazis were doing to Jews, Slavs, gypsies and homosexuals in Europe.

The UN Genocide Convention

Lemkin's new word was quickly adopted. After the defeat of Nazi Germany in 1945, the newly created United Nations Organization set out to make 'genocide' illegal. The UN Convention on the Prevention and Punishment of the Crime of Genocide, passed in December 1948, declared that 'genocide whether committed in time of peace or in time of war, is a crime under international law'.

The Convention defined genocide differently to Lemkin. It described genocide as any of a number of acts 'committed with intent to destroy, in whole or in part, a national, ethnic, racial or religious group'. It said genocide was not only killing members of a group, but also:

- causing them serious bodily or mental harm
- inflicting conditions of life on them that might lead to death
- trying to stop them having children
- taking their children away and giving them to another group to bring up.

A man from the Dinka people of southern Sudan, who today suffer mass human rights abuses.

Many people consider the legal definition of genocide adopted by the UN to be too narrow, because it refers only to the destruction of 'a national, ethnic, racial or religious group'. It excludes the killing of people because they belong to a political party or an economic class – landowners, for example. The Montreal Institute for Genocide Studies suggested a wider definition. They described genocide as any 'form of one-sided mass killing' by a state or other authority. It is in this wider sense that the term genocide is used in this book.

No end to massacre

When the United Nations adopted the Genocide Convention in 1948, some idealists hoped that they might be able to put an end to the era of genocidal massacres. But sadly there have been other cases of mass killings in more recent years, for example those occurring in Bosnia and Rwanda during the 1990s.

The world's great powers, committed to upholding international law, are meant to prevent genocide and prosecute those who carry it out if it occurs. They have generally failed on both counts. This book looks at why genocide happens, what attempts have been made to stop it, who should be held responsible and whether genocide can be prevented in the future.

Soldiers of the Rwandan Patriotic Front look at the skulls of people massacred during the conflict in Rwanda.

Again and again

'Virtually the whole of humankind was of the view that crimes of the magnitude and bestiality of those committed by the Nazi regime would never be repeated. It was the view of most observers that the crimes were unique and a horrible deviation on the road of civilization. That view proved not to be correct ... The hope of "Never again" has become the reality of "Again and again".'

Richard J. Goldstone,
war crime tribunal judge

A Bosnian Muslim woman sits amid the ruins of her home during the genocidal conflict in Bosnia in the 1990s.

Case study

Adolf Hitler's Nazi party came to power in Germany in 1933. The Nazis had a totally racist view of the world. They believed that the Germans belonged to the blond, blue-eyed Aryan race, who were natural masters. They regarded Slavs and Africans as inferior, sub-human peoples, whose only use was as slave workers for the Aryan master race. They thought of gypsies as harmful parasites. But their greatest hatred was reserved for Jewish people.

The Nazis portrayed the Jews as a vile and cunning race, who were plotting to rule the world and enslave the Aryans. This belief, based on historic anti-Semitic prejudices, allowed the Nazis to blame all Germany's recent problems – defeat in the First World War, economic setbacks – on the Jews.

Adolf Hitler with German youths who fitted his 'Aryan' ideal.

The Nazis said the Jews would have to be 'dealt with' if Germany was to be great again. What made the Nazis' attitude to the Jews particularly absurd was that Jewish people were not a clear, distinct group in German society. Most of the half million German Jews thought of themselves simply as Germans. For example, many had fought in the ranks of the German army in the First World War. But between 1933 and 1939, the Nazis gradually isolated the Jews in Germany, barring them from education and jobs. A barrage of propaganda made the German people see the Jews as a dangerous and despicable enemy.

After the Second World War began in 1939, the five million Jews of Poland came under Nazi rule. Jews were forced to wear a yellow star to mark them out and were herded into ghettos – special areas for Jews only. In June 1941 Germany invaded the Soviet Union, and occupied more areas with large Jewish populations, such as Ukraine. The Nazis began to massacre Jews, shooting tens of thousands at a time and burying them in mass graves.

In 1941, the Nazi leadership secretly adopted the Final Solution, a plan to exterminate all the Jews of Europe. Every single Jewish man, woman and child was to die. Extermination camps were set up in occupied Poland, at Auschwitz, Chelmno, Belzec, Sobibor, Treblinka and Majdanek. Millions of Jews were taken there from throughout German-occupied Europe. Most were killed with poison gas.

This photograph was taken in Buchenwald concentration camp when it was liberated by the Allies in 1945.

The Jews were not the only people massacred by the Nazis. Gypsies were targeted for extermination, and millions of Slavs – mostly Poles and Russians – died in the Nazi camps. Thousands of Slav children believed to have Aryan characteristics were stolen from their parents to be brought up as part of the German 'master race'.

But the Jewish people suffered most heavily. In total, an estimated six million Jews were killed by the Nazis, out of a total European Jewish population of eight million. Only the defeat of Nazi Germany by the Allies in 1945 brought the killing to an end. As a deliberate attempt to physically exterminate an entire ethnic group, the Jewish Holocaust is still the most horrific example of genocide to have occurred in the twentieth century.

A memorial wreath and candles mark Crematorium No.1 at Auschwitz, where the bodies were incinerated.

A history of genocide

Massacres are a common feature of world history. Almost 3,000 years ago, the Assyrians triumphantly recorded in stone carvings the massacre, torture, enslavement and mass deportation of the peoples they had conquered. When the ancient Romans defeated the city of Carthage in 146 BC, the whole population was massacred or enslaved. In 1258, Mongol warriors from central Asia slaughtered over 80,000 people after conquering Baghdad.

The mistreatment of minorities who belong to a different race or religion has also occurred throughout history. In Europe in the Middle Ages, for example, Jewish communities lived in fear of massacre by their Christian neighbours. In the Muslim Ottoman Empire, founded in the 1400s, it was the Christians who suffered oppression. Thousands of Christian children in each generation were forcibly taken from their parents by the Ottoman authorities and raised as Muslim slaves.

An ancient Assyrian stone carving showing the victims of a massacre.

Peoples who migrate or expand their territory often crush or drive out other peoples they find in their path. About 2,000 years ago, most of southern Africa was home to the Khoisan. They were hunter-gatherers – people who did not plant crops or rear animals, but lived off game and wild plants. Then, the Bantu peoples migrated into the region. The Bantu were farmers with iron tools and weapons. Within a few centuries, the Khoisan had been driven out, surviving only in dry areas unsuitable for Bantu agriculture.

European expansion

When Europeans began to expand their influence across the globe, from the fifteenth century onward, they brought catastrophe to many of the peoples they encountered in the Americas, Africa and Oceania. In the first century after the Europeans crossed the Atlantic, the native population of the Americas was reduced by at least 90 per cent, through ill-treatment and diseases against which the local peoples had no natural defences. Some peoples, such as the Carib in the West Indies, were almost wiped out.

A Native American man from the Crow tribe. Most European settlers had little regard for Native American life and culture.

Many of the thousands of African slaves shipped to the Americas died during the journey, from starvation and disease.

So many Native Americans died during European expansion that there was a severe shortage of workers for European settlers to employ on their American estates. Between the sixteenth and nineteenth centuries, European traders transported millions of Africans across the Atlantic to be used as slaves. This Atlantic slave trade has often been described as 'genocidal', because of the massive number of deaths it involved and its destructive effect on African cultures.

'Primitive' peoples

It seemed obvious to Europeans that many of the peoples they encountered in other continents were 'primitives', with inferior cultures and technologies. For example, hunter-gatherers such as the Aborigines in Australia or some of the Amazonian Indians had no settled agriculture, in many cases wore few clothes, and had no concept of property. Many Europeans came to regard the extinction of such peoples, along with simple farmers and nomads, as an inevitable consequence of 'progress'. They felt they must either adapt to the modern world, abandoning their traditional ways, or die out.

An Australian Aborigine and cave painting. European settlers often treated 'primitive' art and culture with contempt.

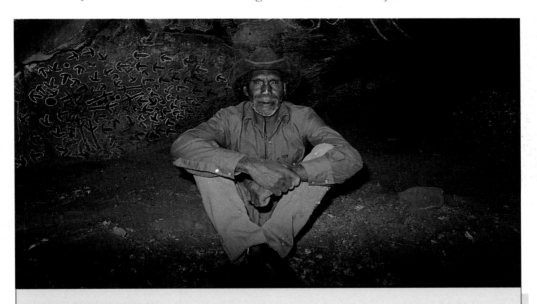

Cultural genocide

'Cultural genocide' is said to happen when the social customs, language, religion and culture of an ethnic group are destroyed. In effect, the group ceases to exist although the individuals who make it up have not been killed. For example, some Aborigines in Australia have claimed that their people were victims of cultural genocide. The Aborigines were not exterminated, but their way of life was destroyed by European settlers.

Civilized European governments on the whole tried to prevent the killing of 'primitive' peoples. But European settlers often hunted them as if they were nuisance animals, and governments usually backed the settlers if the native people tried to fight back. On the island of Tasmania, the native population was hounded to extinction in the nineteenth century. In the same period, many more Native American nations saw their way of life destroyed as the USA continued to spread westward.

This Native American from the Sioux tribe stands in front of a memorial to those of his people who died fighting for the USA in Vietnam.

Talking point

Alfred Russell Wallace, a colleague of Charles Darwin, wrote that the evolutionary struggle for survival 'leads to the inevitable extinction of all those low and mentally undeveloped populations with which the Europeans come into contact'.

Did European settlers have a natural right to destroy the way of life of native peoples such as the Australian Aborigines and the Native Americans?

Hunter-gatherer peoples generally survived into the twentieth century only in remote forest or desert areas. Small numbers of such groups still carry on their traditional way of life today, for example in the forest regions of Brazil and Paraguay, but they are threatened by the destruction of their habitat as forests are cleared, and by attacks from settlers. Other hunter-gatherers and native populations now live on the edge of modern society, on special reservations or poor settlements.

In recent years Native Americans and Aborigines have attempted to reassert their cultural identity. There is a wider awareness of the value of ancient cultures which were so nearly destroyed by genocidal acts.

Founded on genocide

'America was founded on genocide, on the unquestioned assumption of the right of white Europeans to exterminate a resident, technologically backward, colored population in order to take over the continent.'

American author Susan Sontag,
Styles of Radical Will, 1966

A Kayapo Indian boy, dressed for a dance. His people's unique culture is threatened by the Brazilian government's plans to flood large areas of rainforest to create hydro-electricity.

Twentieth-century genocides

The twentieth century justified the invention of the term 'genocide' by the sheer scale of its massacres. An American professor, Rudolph J. Rummel, has estimated the total number of victims of genocide in the twentieth century at 39 million. If all forms of mass murder by the state are taken into account, Rummel's figure rises to 170 million.

A shelter in Bosnia filled with corpses discovered in mass graves after the massacre of Moslems at Srebrenica in 1995.

To try to imagine what this number actually means, Rummel says that if the victims advanced in single file, it would take almost five years for all of them to walk past you.

One of the first, and worst, genocidal acts of the century was the massacre of the Armenian minority in Turkey in 1915–16, during the First World War. The Armenians were hated by many Muslim Turks both because they were Christians and because many of them were prosperous businessmen and traders. They were suspected of supporting Russia, one of Turkey's enemies in the First World War.

These children are Armenian refugees who survived the genocide of 1915.

Almost the entire Armenian population was either massacred or deported in terrible conditions to the wastelands of Syria and Mesopotamia. Hundreds of thousands died on long forced marches or journeys in cattle trucks, without food, shelter, or adequate clothing. In total, about a million Armenians were exterminated.

Revolutionary genocide

Many of the largest massacres of the twentieth century were carried out by governments who wanted to create what they saw as an ideal society. Conducting massive social 'experiments', they felt justified in killing any number of people to achieve their goals.

Communist governments wanted to make a revolutionary change in how people lived, thought and felt. They justified the extreme use of terror by claiming that it was a necessary step towards creating an ideal society free of injustice and want.

Tragedy and statistics

'One man's death is a tragedy;
a million is a statistic.'

Joseph Stalin

Joseph Stalin signs a
death warrant in 1933.

The world's first Communist regime came to power in Russia in 1917. Under its rule, the Russian Empire became the Soviet Union, officially a state in which workers and peasants held power. In practice, however, all power was in the hands of the Communist Party, its bureaucratic officials and its secret police.

Millions of people in the Soviet Union died at the hands of the state, especially during Joseph Stalin's reign as dictator, from 1929 to 1953. Hundreds of thousands were victims of random executions. Tens of millions of people suffered imprisonment in labour camps scattered across the wastelands of Siberia, where death rates were high. Peoples such as the Chechens, Tartars and Kalmyks were subjected to brutal mass deportation from their homelands.

Many of the worst aspects of Stalin's regime were imitated by Mao Zedong's Communist Party, which took power in China after a civil war in 1949. Mao's victims were targeted not by race but by class. Landowners and businessmen were massacred because they were believed to be standing in the way of a new classless society. The Cultural Revolution of 1966, in which young people were encouraged by Mao to attack educated adults and officials, led to deaths on a vast scale.

It is difficult to estimate the number of genocide victims in the twentieth century. Many deaths were covered up or unrecorded. There are also problems telling one kind of killing from another – what is genocide and what is not? For example, it is difficult to say how many of the tens of millions of people killed by the state in the Soviet Union and Communist China were victims of genocide.

Mao Zedong's army in Beijing in 1968. They hold up the Little Red Book which contained Mao's ideas.

The legacy of Pol Pot

'Pol Pot's legacy is a continuing cancer at the heart of Cambodia. The failure to bring Pol Pot and his fellow Khmer Rouge commanders to justice is reflected in ongoing human rights violations in Cambodia. The spectre of political killings still stalks Cambodia today. Perpetrators of human rights abuses still escape the courts with impunity and ordinary people are still not free from fear. Until truth and justice become a reality in Cambodia, the country will be trapped in a cycle of despair.

Pol Pot was not the only architect of Cambodia's killing fields ... many other senior Khmer Rouge cadres remain free and unpunished. They should not be allowed to escape justice.'

Amnesty International, after the death of Pol Pot in 1998

Cambodian killing fields

The most extreme of all Communist governments came to power in Cambodia, a state in south-east Asia, in 1975. A movement called the Khmer Rouge won control of the country after its peasant army had fought a guerrilla war against a government backed by the USA. The leaders of the Khmer Rouge, including the notorious Pol Pot, believed that only a total revolution could create a society free of corruption and Western capitalist influence.

Their first act on seizing power was to drive almost the entire population of the capital, Phnom Penh, into the countryside. They were then subjected to total collectivization – there was no private property, people were only allowed to eat in canteens, and everyone except the Khmer Rouge themselves had to perform relentless work in the fields from dawn until dusk.

Killing for a new social order

'A fascinating revolution for all who aspire to a new social order. A terrifying one, for all who have any respect for human beings.'

François Ponchaud,
French author writing about
the Khmer Rouge revolution
in Cambodia

Many city folk, unused to manual work and subjected to brutal treatment by Khmer Rouge guards, died of exhaustion or disease. Tens of thousands of people who were believed to be teachers, doctors or students were murdered by young Khmer Rouge guerrillas.

The Cambodian regime gives a chilling insight into how any group can be randomly selected for genocidal attack. Those whom the Khmer Rouge believed should be exterminated included anyone who wore glasses, and anyone who spoke a foreign language. Victims were usually struck with a spade on the back of the skull, and buried in mass graves.

Skulls and bones from the 'killing fields' of Cambodia.

The Khmer Rouge also carried out a genocidal campaign against Muslim tribespeople in Cambodia, called the Cham. The total death toll under Khmer Rouge rule, which lasted less than four years, is estimated at between a sixth and a third of the Cambodian population.

Colonial legacies

In the first half of the twentieth century, much of the world was ruled by Britain, France and other European countries. After 1945, these colonial empires began to fall apart. Many of the countries that achieved independence from colonial rule had a mix of different ethnic groups within their new borders. This situation led to acts of mass killing.

When Pakistan became independent in 1947, it was divided into East and West Pakistan. The two regions were separated by more than 1,000 kilometres of Indian territory, and had little in common. Not surprisingly, this arrangement did not work. In 1971, the Pakistani army carried out widespread massacres of the Bengali population of East Pakistan, in an attempt to stop the country declaring independence as Bangladesh.

Onlookers at the grave of over 100 academic leaders in Bangladesh in 1971. Educated people were the targets for mass killing in Cambodia, China and Bangladesh.

In Africa, the new states created when colonial rule ended bore no relation to the nature of the local populations. Many states contained a patchwork of different ethnic groups, and suffered from severe economic and political problems. All of these conditions encouraged the possibility of genocide.

In Nigeria, the Ibo were massacred in the 1960s. In Sudan, the northern Muslims who rule the country have waged war on southern tribespeople such as the Dinka for decades. When the dictator Idi Amin ruled Uganda in the 1970s, around 300,000 people were killed. In Burundi and Rwanda, hundreds of thousands of people have been victims of genocide.

A young survivor of genocide in Rwanda in 1994.

Case study

In 1884, as part of the division of Africa between European colonial powers, Germany took over the vast territory of South West Africa (now called Namibia). This included the lands inhabited by the Herero people, who lived by herding cattle. The Herero soon found themselves being pushed out by German settlers who moved on to their land.

In 1904, the Herero revolted against German rule. The Germans sent General Lothar von Trotta to put down the uprising. Trotta was totally ruthless. He easily defeated the Herero army and forced the warriors to retreat into the desert, where most died of thirst.

But Trotta was not content with a military victory. He issued an order that said: 'Inside German territory every Herero tribesman, armed or unarmed, with or without cattle, will be shot.' In the months that followed, German soldiers and armed settlers carried out Trotta's order to the letter. Four out of every five Herero had been killed by the time the massacres came to an end.

German troops in South West Africa at the time of the Herero genocide.

Genocide in the 1990s

The history of mass killing shows no sign of coming to an end. In Iraq since the 1980s, the Kurdish people have been subject to massacre and poison gas attacks by the forces of the dictator Saddam Hussein. In African states such as Sudan and Burundi, mass killing remains a fact of life.

A Jewish prisoner in Buchenwald camp in 1945 (bottom), and a prisoner in a Serbian camp in Bosnia fifty years later. Circumstances are very different, but inhumanity continues.

Appalling atrocities returned to Europe in the 1990s, when the Communist state of Yugoslavia broke up into small states. In an attempt to control as much of the former Yugoslavia as possible, various groups engaged in 'ethnic cleansing'. This terribly clinical term describes the process by which areas inhabited by mixed communities of Serbs, Croats and Muslims were transformed into areas with a single ethnic identity. Massacre and forced deportation were widely used to clear out the unwanted minorities, especially by the Serbs in Bosnia. In 1998, killings of Albanians and Serbs escalated again in Kosovo.

At the end of the Second World War, when the horrors of Nazi racial policies had become known, world leaders had promised to try to ensure that such a thing would never happen again. Although the massacres in Bosnia were on a smaller scale than the Nazi Holocaust, they reminded people that 'Never again' had become 'Again and again'.

Causes of genocide

Why do human beings commit genocidal massacres? Since genocide has happened throughout history, it might seem obvious to explain it as a fact of human nature. Clearly, if human beings did not have aggressive and destructive urges that drive them to fight and sometimes kill one another, genocide would never happen.

Some biologists have argued that human beings evolved as tight-knit bands of close relatives. These bands fought to defend their territory against all outsiders, and to extend their territory at the expense of other bands. According to this argument, to have different groups of humans living on the same territory and in the same society is unnatural. It consequently causes those humans to commit acts of aggression, and ultimately genocide.

But in the course of history, many complex human societies have developed and flourished in which different ethnic groups have co-operated and lived side by side. In other words, it is a fact that if you put human beings of different races or ethnic groups together in the same country or state, they do not automatically turn to massacring one another.

Every genocide or massacre is different. But there are some basic factors that make genocide more likely to occur.

> ## Flawed human nature
> 'If one looks with a cold eye at the mess man has made of his history, it is difficult to avoid the conclusion that he has been afflicted by some built-in mental disorder which drives him towards self-destruction.'
>
> Arthur Koestler,
> British author, 1968

An armed woman in Bosnia. Many people who would not normally use violence are drawn into armed conflicts.

Historical grievances

Firstly, and most obviously, genocide thrives on historic ethnic and religious hatreds and prejudices. For example, the Serbs and Croats who lived together in the former Yugoslavia had been divided throughout their history by religion. The Serbs were Orthodox Christians and the Croats were Catholics.

After Yugoslavia was founded in 1918, the Croats resented the fact that it was dominated by the Serbs. Relations between the two nations were especially embittered by the events of the Second World War, when Croatia sided with the Nazi Germans. Many Serbs died in Croatian concentration camps. After the break-up of Yugoslavia in 1991, these historical grievances and resentments all returned to the surface. The years of growing hatred culminated in massacres on both sides.

Where ethnic hatreds and historic grievances exist, there is a powder keg waiting to explode. The spark for the explosion may be provided by some political crisis – a war, an attempt to overthrow a government, an invasion, a breakdown of order, or even some well-meaning attempt at political reform. This can trigger communal violence that escalates to horrific levels.

Croatian soldiers show their enthusiasm for the struggle against Serbia in the Bosnian war.

Case study

Rwanda and Burundi are neighbouring states in central Africa. In both countries there is a majority of Hutu people, who are traditionally settled farmers. There is a minority of Tutsi people, who are traditionally cattle-herders and warriors.

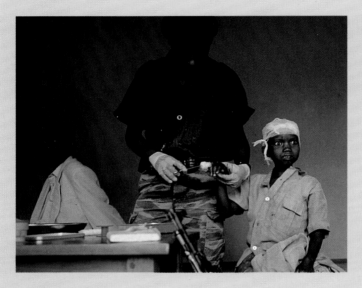

An injured Hutu boy. Many victims in Rwanda suffered head wounds from machete blows.

The Hutu and Tutsi had, on the whole, lived together peacefully until Burundi and Rwanda became independent countries in 1962. After independence, political leaders in both countries based their power on appeals to ethnic loyalty.

In Burundi, a Tutsi government centred all power and privilege in the hands of the Tutsi minority. Political tensions spilled over into genocidal massacres in 1972–73. After a failed Hutu uprising, in which many Tutsi were murdered, the Tutsi-dominated army and paramilitaries massacred hundreds of thousands of Hutu.

There were further killings of Hutu in Burundi in 1988. Then, a Hutu president was elected in a breakthrough for democracy. But this only provoked Tutsi extremists into attempting a coup in late 1993, sparking still more large-scale killings. Each new massacre increased the fear and hostility that were tearing the region apart.

In Rwanda, it was the Hutus who formed the government. They took power and discriminated against the Tutsi minority. In 1990, a civil war began in which Tutsi rebels took on the Hutu government.

In April 1994, the presidents of Rwanda and Burundi were killed in a plane crash after attending peace talks. In Rwanda, the Hutu extremists immediately began wholesale massacres of Tutsi and of moderate Hutu opponents of the regime. The Hutu militias that carried out the killings were highly organized and had been carefully prepared for their role by the Hutu government. Half a million people are believed to have lost their lives.

Hutu refugees returning to their homes, after two years in Zaire.

In July 1994, Tutsi rebel forces gained control of Rwanda. The Hutu militias and millions of ordinary Hutu people fled to refugee camps outside the country, fearing reprisals from the new rulers. Most Hutus returned to their homes at the end of 1996.

Why promote genocide?

Governments promote genocide for the following reasons:

- To use the victims as scapegoats: they are blamed for problems such as defeat in war, unemployment and poverty. Attacking them deflects anger away from the government.
- To assert total power: authoritarian governments may view the minority as a threat to their total dominance of society.
- To find a quick solution: mass killing is seen as a quick answer to the problems of different ethnic groups living together.
- Creating solidarity: genocide can help strengthen a sense of group identity, binding together those who have taken part.

A Khmer Rouge soldier pictured in 1975.

Exploiting hatred

True genocide is not something which happens spontaneously, as a simple flaring up of hatred between different races or groups. Although there are sometimes 'race riots' in which many people are killed, massacres on a large scale over a period of time need a good degree of organization, planning, and leadership.

Genocide usually only happens when dictators, governments or political movements exploit and encourage prejudice and hatred for their own ends. In Cambodia, for example, the Khmer Rouge exploited a genuine hostility felt by peasants towards well-off townspeople. To the peasants, townspeople meant the moneylender who charged them high interest or the trader who paid low prices for their crops. The Khmer Rouge leaders portrayed townspeople as idle parasites, preying on the hard-working peasant. Encouraged in their prejudice, the peasants became a part of the Khmer Rouge policy which led to mass killing.

Dehumanization

All people accept a basic rule that you do not normally kill other human beings. So before genocide can take place, the victims have to be 'dehumanized' – they must become less than human beings in the eyes of those who are going to carry out or accept the killings. When the victims are not seen as real, full humans, killing them does not feel like murder, and so is not prohibited.

All forms of ethnic and racial hatred or prejudice tend to be dehumanizing. If people are habitually referred to by abusive and insulting words, or are the constant object of racist jokes or stories, they will gradually cease to seem completely human.

Political movements or governments can encourage dehumanization through propaganda. For example, the Jews were repeatedly described by the Nazis as an infection, as animals, as vile monsters. Ordinary German people became used to the idea that Jews were not really people. They could therefore accept inhuman treatment of them.

When Jews were publicly humiliated by the Nazis – for example, by being made to scrub pavements with toothbrushes – this degradation made them seem even less human in the eyes of bystanders who witnessed it.

Abuse leads to killing

'The educated Northerners spoke of the Ibo as vermin, criminals, money-grabbers, and sub-humans without genuine culture ... [This] talking about a minority group in non-human terms ... seems essential to provide some kind of justification for dealing with other human beings as one would treat dangerous animals – exterminate them.'

Colin Legum, the *Observer*, talking about dehumanization and mass killing in Nigeria in 1966

Elderly Jews in Vienna are forced to scrub the streets by Nazi soldiers in 1938.

Mistreatment and isolation

Ill-treatment itself is dehumanizing. Psychologists have observed that when people see a group being treated badly, they tend to feel that somehow the victims must deserve it.

In a case like the Holocaust, the people targeted for genocide are connected to members of the wider community as friends, workmates, neighbours, even relatives by marriage. Genocide cannot happen until they have been isolated and marked out. The Nazi government spent years separating Jewish people from the rest of the population, stopping them marrying or mixing with non-Jews. Eventually, the Nazis forced Jews to wear a yellow star and to live in ghettos completely apart from non-Jews. This separation made their extermination possible.

Them and us

'These concentration camp guards, though they lived in the same physical environments as their victims, nevertheless managed to build so immense a social distance between 'them' and 'us' that they perceive their victims as not belonging to the same human race.'

Lewis A. Coser, sociologist, talking about guards in Nazi death camps

A Jewish couple in Budapest forced by Nazis to wear the Star of David.

Elite killers

Governments engaged in genocide often employ special killing squads. These 'elite' units are trained to see it as their mission to crush the victim group. Such units include the SS (*SchutzStaffel*) in Nazi Germany and the Hutu militias in Rwanda. In such squads, all traces of pity or human feeling are repressed as 'weakness'. The members are trained to believe absolutely in a world view that sees the genocide as necessary and good. They are given a strong sense of group loyalty that is strengthened by the crimes they commit – they become a brotherhood bound together by the blood they have spilt.

However, genocides also involve the participation of a wide cross-section of the civilian population. Many of the Germans who massacred Jews were not members of the SS. Reserve Police Battalion 101, made up of ordinary, middle-aged, working-class conscripts, killed around 83,000 Jews in cold blood between 1942 and 1945. These were people who, under ordinary circumstances, would have been well-behaved, harmless citizens. This is perhaps one of the most frightening aspects of genocide.

> **Talking point**
>
> 'If the men of Reserve Police Battalion 101 could become killers under such circumstances, what group of men cannot?'
>
> Christopher Browning, historian, writing about the Nazi genocide
>
> Do you believe that absolutely anyone is capable of taking part in genocide?

Young Hutu militiamen. They were trained in obedience, ruthlessness and hatred of the Tutsis.

Technology and genocide

Modern technology has made killing more efficient and this has tended to increase the scale of genocides. The Nazi gas chambers at Auschwitz were efficient killing factories, capable of 'processing' thousands of victims in a few hours. But people who wish to kill can always find a means. The simplest weapons can be used to kill hundreds of thousands – for example, shovels in Cambodia or machetes in Rwanda.

A collection of machetes used for murder in the Rwandan genocide.

Authoritarian governments

The conditions for genocide are hard to create in an open, democratic society. Governments which carry out genocide are normally authoritarian. They encourage a strong sense of discipline and unquestioning obedience in their people. They often have secret police who create a general atmosphere of fear. This makes people more ready to support or ignore genocide. The majority of people become bystanders, unready to intervene whatever they may think of what is going on.

Genocide is normally cloaked in secrecy. The killers make desperate efforts to cover up their acts. Fear is used to enforce secrecy. If people dare not ask questions about what is going on around them – about people who suddenly disappear in the night or trainloads of prisoners being carried to unknown destinations – committing genocide becomes a much easier task.

Yet genocide is never a total secret. Events on such a scale are inevitably known to many. The question remains, how is it possible for such inhuman crimes to be carried out without anyone stopping them or, usually, anyone being punished?

Investigators uncover a mass grave in Bosnia. The killers had hoped that the bodies would never be found.

Responses to genocide

When the United Nations adopted the Convention on Genocide in 1948, the international community effectively declared genocide illegal. Yet the world powers continue to allow genocide to happen.

In some cases, intervention to stop genocide might be impossible without starting a major war. Most of the world may disapprove of China's occupation of Tibet and its mistreatment of the Tibetan people. Some people believe the only effective way to stop what China is doing would be to fight a war with China, yet this might lead to death and destruction on a massive scale.

A Tibetan woman prays, watched over by Chinese soldiers with orders to crush any sign of resistance to Chinese rule.

But many of the mass killings in recent years, including those in Rwanda and Bosnia, have occurred in relatively weak countries, where diplomatic pressure or military intervention backed by major world powers was a serious possibility. Why have outside powers or organizations, including the UN, been so slow and reluctant to act?

The knowledge gap

The first problem in responding to genocide is finding out for certain that it is happening. Governments that are engaged in genocide do not advertise the fact. They generally try to prevent journalists or foreign observers seeing what is happening. They also issue public denials when they are accused.

The outside world may first find out about genocide from the accounts given by refugees fleeing the massacres. Organizations such as Amnesty International monitor what is happening in countries where genocide is a possibility, and try to alert world opinion when massacres take place. Graphic photographs or television news footage are the quickest and surest way to overcome public apathy. For example, a famous photo of a starving prisoner in a Serbian prison camp, published in 1992 (shown on page 25), made many people in the West support military intervention in the Bosnian crisis.

A Bosnian Serb officer tries to stop a foreign TV cameraman filming at Sarajevo Airport.

But reports of genocide are often dismissed. There is a tendency not to believe genocide is happening, because it seems too extreme to be possible. Many sources of information on genocide, such as refugees, are regarded as biased and therefore unreliable. By the time international observers have established beyond doubt that genocide is taking place, hundreds of thousands of people may already have died.

Holding back

Even when it is clear that genocide is taking place, as in the case of Rwanda in 1994, there is still a reluctance to intervene. Governments all across the world have a strong belief in national sovereignty – meaning that the government of a country has the power to decide what is done within that country. Genocide is thus seen as an 'internal affair' that should not be the concern of foreign powers.

Intervention

There are a number of different measures the major powers can take if they do decide to follow a policy of intervention. At the lowest level, diplomatic protests can be made, asking the government concerned to stop its activities. This is the easiest form of action to agree on, but often the least effective.

Alternatively, what is happening can be exposed publicly, and the country can receive international condemnation. Such an approach can create far greater pressure.

The UN Secretary General Kofi Annan in 1998, visiting a memorial to the 1994 Rwandan genocide victims. Annan received a cold and hostile welcome in Rwanda, because of the failure of the UN to intervene and stop the genocides.

Sanctions

The international community can also choose to impose economic and other sanctions against the offending state – for example, by banning the sale of arms to the state concerned, banning trade with it, or withdrawing economic aid.

This is a form of pressure that can have some impact. But it is slow to take effect and may simply increase the guilty country's determination to act as it chooses. It may also hurt the country's people, without changing the policy of its leaders.

Military force

By far the most radical intervention is to send in a military force, but this is very hazardous. Governments are often reluctant to do it. They fear the long-term and expensive entanglement in a foreign country that military intervention might involve. Getting agreement on joint military action is also very difficult.

Civilians and blue-helmeted UN soldiers come under sniper fire in Bosnia. UN military intervention failed to stop the fighting.

Many people might be killed in a military action intended to save lives. Turmoil and chaos may result, unless the intervening powers have a clear plan to install a new government or provide a settlement of the situation.

Pursuing self-interest

Governments generally pursue their own country's self-interest, rather than idealistic goals such as upholding human rights. This is, in a sense, what national governments are for. The conflicting interests of different states inevitably make any form of intervention extremely complicated.

In Bosnia, the German government tended to support the Croats, with whom it had a close relationship. Many other European countries were suspicious of Croatia. Russia had historic links with the Serbs, and suspected that Western accusations of Serb atrocities were politically motivated. Achieving agreement on joint action by the major powers was very difficult.

Failure to intervene

'Half a million Jews were murdered in Auschwitz between March and November 1944 ... yet the railway lines leading to the death camps were never targeted.'

Alain Destexhe, French human rights worker, comparing the lack of intervention in Rwanda with the Holocaust

Bosnian Muslims are evacuated, watched by UN troops, after the failure of UN intervention to prevent Serb attacks.

In Rwanda, France had close economic and military links with the Hutu-dominated government of Rwanda. This created a problem for co-ordinating international action against the Hutu even after genocidal killings began.

In both Bosnia and Rwanda, matters were further complicated by the fact that no side in the conflicts was completely innocent. All sides in Bosnia carried out ethnic cleansing to some degree. In Rwanda, both the Tutsi and the Hutu were responsible for massacres. This made it more difficult to persuade the international community that intervention against those mainly responsible for the atrocities – the Serbs in Bosnia and the Hutu in Rwanda – was justified.

UN soldiers in Rwanda. They did not intervene to stop the killing.

Against intervention

It might seem obvious that if a country has the power to send in armed forces to stop genocide happening, it should do so. But there are strong arguments against military intervention:

- The political situations in which genocides happen are complicated, and military intervention can make the situation worse.
- The use of force should be avoided in international affairs, whatever the cause.
- A country's internal affairs are its own business, for better or for worse.
- If major powers sent in their armies every time a country offended against human rights, it would lead to endless wars.

Self-interest leads to intervention

Sometimes, the pursuit of self-interest can lead a government to intervene on its own to stop massacres. This happened when India invaded Bangladesh in 1971, halting the massacres of Bengalis by the Pakistani army. It also happened when the Vietnamese invaded Cambodia and overthrew the Khmer Rouge government in 1979.

In both these cases, the intervention was motivated not by concern for human rights, but by complex political ambitions. The Vietnamese were widely condemned as aggressors for their action. This created a bizarre situation in which countries such as the USA and Britain supported the genocidal Khmer Rouge against the Vietnamese.

The problems of the UN

The United Nations Organization has generally been ineffectual in the face of genocide. The UN is, after all, only made up of representatives of individual governments. If those governments do not agree on action, there is nothing the UN can do.

Until the late 1980s, the UN was often paralysed by the Cold War. With the USA and its allies in opposition to the Soviet Union, international co-operation was almost impossible. The end of the Cold War has made it easier for the major powers to work together. This was demonstrated by Russian support for the NATO-led peacekeeping force which was sent to Bosnia in 1996.

Disillusioned with the UN

'The performance of the United Nations Organization in the suppression of the crime of genocide is deeply disillusioning, particularly against the background of the humanitarian ideals which inspired its founding ... But of course the United Nations is not a humanitarian, but a political, organization, and its humanitarian goals are at the play of political forces ...'

Leo Kuper,
South African sociologist

UN interventions have often been ineffective because of the UN's commitment to remaining completely neutral in a conflict. In practice, it is almost impossible not to take sides if you want to stop genocide. In the Bosnian crisis, for example, the United Nations sent in a 'Protection Force' to stop massacres and protect food supplies. But the UN troops had orders not to become involved in the Bosnian civil war. They were ordered not to fight except in self-defence. The result was that 'ethnic cleansing' continued, while UN forces stood aside.

The UN has on the whole been ready to take a more assertive line on genocide in recent years. One sign of this has been the creation of the first international tribunals since the 1940s to put people on trial for genocide, war crimes and acts against humanity.

Peacekeepers, like this British UN soldier in Bosnia, often receive a warm welcome from frightened local people.

Case study

Bosnia is an area of former Yugoslavia with a mixed population of Muslims, Serbs and Croats. In 1992, Bosnian Muslims and Croats declared Bosnia independent. This was opposed by Bosnian Serbs, and a civil war started. The United Nations sent in a 'Protection Force'.

In 1993, the United Nations declared a safe haven around the Bosnian town of Srebrenica. By 1995, Srebrenica's population of about 15,000 Muslims had been joined by around 25,000 refugees. UN troops from the Netherlands manned a perimeter around the safe haven.

As Bosnian Serb pressure on Srebrenica mounted through the summer of 1995, the UN leadership refused to authorize military action. In mid-July, the Serbs advanced on Srebrenica. Lacking clear instructions, the Dutch UN soldiers failed to put up any resistance. On 11 July, they drove away and allowed the Serbs to take over.

The defenceless Muslim population was subjected to what has been called the worst single atrocity in Europe since the end of the Second World War. The Serbs loaded Muslim men on to trucks and drove them to a killing ground where they were shot. The bodies were buried in mass graves. The number of dead is estimated at between 6,000 and 8,000.

Bosnian Muslim children are moved away from Srebrenica to safety.

Genocide on trial

In 1945, an International Military Tribunal was set up in Nuremberg to try Nazi leaders. This was the first international attempt to prosecute individuals for war crimes and crimes against humanity. For the next half century, however, national governments were left to investigate and prosecute their own citizens. Despite the existence of the UN Convention declaring genocide illegal, no effort was made to enforce that law at international level.

In 1995, however, in rapid succession the International Criminal Tribunal for Former Yugoslavia and the International Criminal Tribunal for Rwanda were set up by the United Nations. In 1998, the international community agreed the statute for a permanent International Criminal Court, to try crimes against humanity. Only time will tell if the court can prove effective.

Otto Ohlendorf, a general in the SS, is sentenced at the Nuremberg trials.

Case study

At Nuremberg in 1945–6, twenty-four leading Nazis, including Hermann Goering and Rudolf Hess, were tried by an International Military Tribunal. The court was set up by the powers that had just defeated Germany – the USA, the Soviet Union, Britain and France.

The Nazi leaders were accused of 'crimes against peace', 'war crimes' and 'crimes against humanity'. Among the charges against the defendants were that they had 'conducted deliberate and systematic genocide ... in order to destroy particular races and classes of people and national, racial, or religious groups, particularly Jews, Poles and gypsies ...'

There were doubts in many people's minds about the legality of the trials. However, most agreed with Justice Jackson, the chief US prosecutor, that Nazi crimes were 'so malignant and so devastating that civilization cannot tolerate their being ignored'.

The trials paraded Nazi atrocities before the eyes of the world. Twelve Nazis were sentenced to death, and ten of these were actually executed. Lesser Nazis were prosecuted in subsequent trials, although many received only light sentences. Most were never arrested at all and resumed normal lives.

The leading Nazi war criminals on trial at Nuremberg.

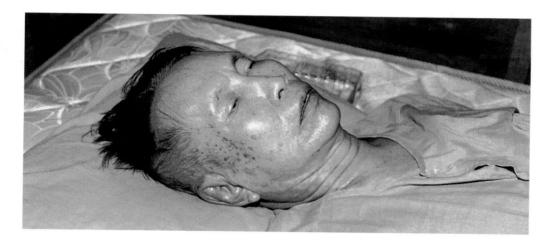

Who is guilty?

Trials immediately raise the question of who is truly responsible for genocide. Is it the person who pulls the trigger or swings the machete? Or is it the people who plan and organize the massacres? Many thousands of ordinary people take part in genocide. Should they all be prosecuted?

The government of West Germany officially accepted collective guilt for the Holocaust, paying compensation to the state of Israel as representative of the Jewish people. But many individuals – such as railway officials who organized the trains that took Jews to the gas chambers, or civil servants who had organized the paperwork for the massacres – did not feel any personal responsibility for the killings.

Even those who directly carry out genocidal massacres have rarely shown any signs of feeling guilt. The massacres are generally accompanied by a powerful feeling of righteousness. Pol Pot, the Cambodian Khmer Rouge leader most responsible for the 'killing fields', died in 1998 still defending the rightness of what he had done.

Pol Pot, the man most responsible for the Cambodian 'killing fields', died in 1998. His body was exhibited to journalists.

General Ratko Mladic (left)
and Radovan Karadzic,
Bosnian Serb leaders
indicted for ordering
genocide.

Leaders and followers

Trying the leaders responsible for genocide can be extremely difficult. The tribunals for former Yugoslavia and Rwanda have had little success in finding and arresting the individuals they want to put on trial. The Bosnian Serb leaders Radovan Karadzic and General Ratko Mladic were the most prominent people accused by the Tribunal for Former Yugoslavia, but neither had been seized two years after international arrest warrants were issued.

Inevitably, the tribunals find themselves prosecuting people lower down the chain of command. Prosecutors have justified the pursuit of less important individuals by saying that it helps to build up evidence against the main criminals who planned and ordered the killings.

It is often argued that only those giving orders should be held responsible; and that it is wrong to prosecute people who were obeying orders. This was discounted during the Nuremberg trials, which established the principle that a soldier had a duty to disobey an order under certain extreme conditions.

Obeying orders?

Former SS officer Albert Hartl said he knew 'of no instance in which refusal to take part in the shooting of Jews resulted in anyone being sent to a concentration camp or being sentenced to death.'

Military training, however, is designed to ensure that individuals obey orders without thinking about their personal feelings. It has been observed that people in a group – whether a military formation or a civilian mob – will do things which their conscience and morality would not let them do alone.

Should even bystanders feel a sense of guilt? Many Germans who had watched the Jews disappear from their towns and cities felt no guilt. They justified themselves by saying they did not know what was happening or had no power to intervene.

Who can judge?

Who has the right to judge? The judges at the Nuremberg trials were from Britain, which had bombed Dresden killing around 70,000 civilians; the USA which had dropped atom bombs on Hiroshima and Nagasaki killing at least 100,000 civilians; and the Soviet Union which had massacred millions of its own people. Because they had won the war, they were able to judge the Germans. If they had lost, would they themselves have been accused of war crimes?

The Japanese city of Hiroshima, destroyed by an atom bomb in 1945.

Lord Shawcross, the chief British prosecutor at the Nuremberg trials, wrote in his memoirs that he feared 'by their own conduct of the war, the Allies had lost the moral authority to conduct the trial'.

It should also be remembered that governments responsible for genocide often receive economic support and military supplies from the very countries which later seek to prosecute them for their crimes.

Do trials work?

Critics of trials for crimes against humanity have pointed out that the process is always bound up with politics. After all, only the victors or the more powerful side in a conflict are ever in a position to try people for genocide. Some people feel that trials are a disguise for revenge against defeated enemies.

It is fundamental to decide if prosecution reduces the chance of future genocides. Supporters of human rights trials claim they act as a deterrent. They make people realize that acts of genocide will be punished. Trials are also said to restore a sense of moral order. It is claimed that just punishment can break the cycle of genocide, making it less likely that the victims of one genocide will in turn seek genocidal revenge on their persecutors.

Opponents of prosecutions believe that trials inevitably create a sense of grievance which can actually fuel future conflicts.

Even-handed

'The Tribunal cannot and must not take sides in the conflict, and we have taken great care not to do so. Our policy is to be even-handed in the sense that we will treat similar crimes in a similar way, irrespective of the identity of the perpetrators.'

Richard J Goldstone,
chief prosecutor of the
International Tribunal on War
Crimes in the former Yugoslavia

A Rwandan schoolgirl visits her old classroom, scene of a massacre in 1994. Should the killers face trial?

Truth and reconciliation

An alternative to trials is the appointment of a 'Truth and Reconciliation Commission', an approach adopted by Nelson Mandela's South African government, as well as in Chile and El Salvador in the 1990s. The Commission publicly investigates the crimes committed by all sides in a past conflict. All the people taking part are guaranteed freedom from prosecution, as a way of encouraging them to speak out. This breaks the cycle of punishment and renewed bitterness.

The South African Truth and Reconciliation Commission, headed by Desmond Tutu, has been entrusted with uncovering the truth about crimes committed under the white-only rule of apartheid in South Africa. It has enabled, for example, the families of those killed while in the custody of the South African police to learn the details of their relatives' deaths and confront their murderers. Yet many people feel that the absence of prosecution for such crimes leaves a sense of injustice.

> ### Talking point
>
> 'It is essential for the world to see the prosecution of genocidal criminals, not least in order to deter extremists elsewhere who might be contemplating similar crimes.'
>
> African Rights,
> after the Rwandan genocide, 1994
>
> 'If you want to lead a normal life, you must forget. Otherwise those wild snakes freed from their box will poison public life for years to come.'
>
> Jorge Semprun, Spanish writer,
> opposing prosecution for political crimes
>
> Who is right?

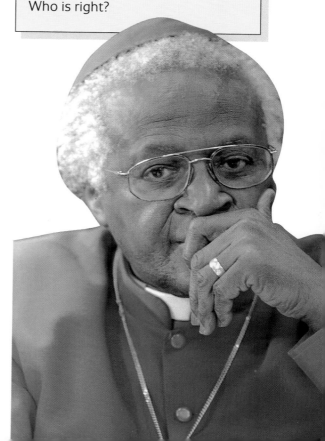

Archbishop Desmond Tutu at a hearing of the Truth and Reconciliation Commission.

Can genocide be avoided?

Talking point

'Few people can be happy unless they hate some other person, nation or creed.'

Bertrand Russell, British philosopher

Was he right?

At risk

In the mid-1990s, experts Barbara Harff and Ted Robert Gurr drew up a list of minorities worldwide that they thought most at risk from potential genocides. They included:

Europe
- Serbs in Croatia
- Muslims in Serb-controlled areas of Bosnia
- Albanians in the Kosovo region of Serb-controlled former Yugoslavia

Asia
- Muslims in Indian-ruled Kashmir
- Tibetans under Chinese rule
- Timorese under Indonesian rule
- Kurds in Iraq

Africa
- Ovimbundu in Angola
- Hutu in Burundi
- Tuareg in Mali and Niger
- Dinka, Nuba, and Shilluk people in Sudan

The Americas
- Mayans in Guatemala
- Native peoples of the Brazilian rainforest

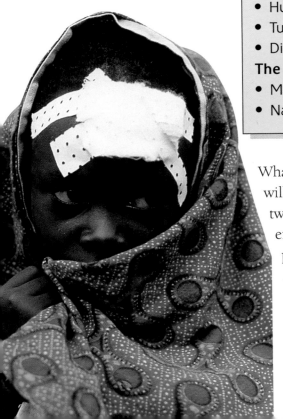

At risk – an injured Rwandan girl at an orphanage.

What are the chances that the twenty-first century will be free of genocide? The experience of the twentieth century has, to say the least, not been encouraging. But, just possibly, humans may prove capable of learning from their past. Although the 1990s have seen appalling massacres, they have also been a time when democracy has spread to new countries, such as South Africa, and international pressure on countries abusing human rights has increased.

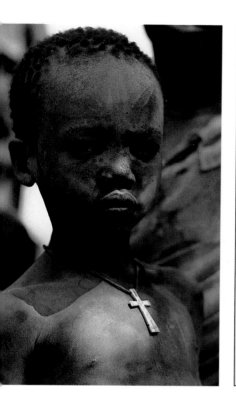

At risk – a Christian Dinka boy. The Dinka of southern Sudan are a target for attacks by government-backed militias.

Automatic intervention

Some experts have suggested that a 'tripwire' is needed to trigger swift action to halt genocide. They argue that a figure should be set for the number of deaths that would be considered intolerable – say, 50,000. Once expert observers had estimated that 50,000 people had died in massacres, the UN would be obliged to send in military force immediately to halt the killings. Those who support such an automatic threshold argue that it would prevent the endless discussions and hesitations that at present allow hundreds of thousands to die while nothing is done.

Preventing genocide

Some experts believe that we now have the ability to anticipate genocide and thus to intervene early to prevent it. Some of the warning signs are well known; for example, the use of dehumanizing propaganda against a minority group, and the isolation of a possible target group from the rest of the population.

There are organizations which campaign against genocide, such as Amnesty International. They monitor dangerous situations around the world. Where they recognize a danger of genocide, the international community, acting through the UN, could intervene before the killing starts. They could even deploy peacekeeping forces in potential trouble spots.

A multiracial world

In the longer term, what sort of world do we need to build to prevent genocide happening again? The solution of having everyone live in societies made up of single ethnic groups is simply not practicable. For better or for worse, we are going to live in multiracial, multicultural societies. How, then, can different peoples live side by side and respect one another's culture and humanity?

One form of multiracial society that has been common in history works by recognizing and accepting the importance of distinct ethnic groups. It tries to create a balanced arrangement where different groups have a role to play while remaining separate and distinct.

At risk – a Kayapo Indian boy in the Brazilian rainforest.

Hope for the future

'I have cherished the ideal of a democratic and free society in which all persons live together in harmony and with equal opportunities ... if needs be it is an ideal for which I am prepared to die.'

Nelson Mandela, when sentenced to life imprisonment in 1964

Such balanced societies can be unstable, however. Lebanon, in the Middle East, had an elaborate arrangement to involve its many different ethnic and religious communities in running the country. For example, a Christian was always president and a Muslim was vice-president. But when the arrangement broke down in the 1970s, a long and destructive civil war resulted.

An alternative form of multiracial society is based on integration. In societies such as Britain and the USA, the law makes no distinction between ethnic groups. Officially, there are only individual citizens. The ethnic identity of individuals is respected, in the sense that the law defends their right to follow their own beliefs and customs. But ethnic identity is blurred, because individuals from different groups belong to the same schools, workplaces, sports clubs and so on.

Political parties in such societies are not set up on racial grounds. So, all political leaders compete for the votes of all ethnic groups. Ideally, they have no interest in advocating racism.

An armed boy in Lebanon, which was reduced to ruins by fighting between different ethnic and religious groups.

Young Bosnian refugees, at risk from ethnic conflict.

Case study

One of the most promising examples of progress in avoiding genocidal conflict in recent years has come from South Africa. From the 1940s to the 1990s, a white government imposed an apartheid regime in South Africa. Power and privilege were kept in the hands of the white minority. Many whites believed that the only alternative to apartheid would be a genocidal uprising by the African majority that would drown the whites in a sea of blood.

South African president Nelson Mandela, a committed believer in a multicultural future.

In 1990, however, the South African leader F. W. de Klerk decided reform was needed. He released the African National Congress (ANC) leader Nelson Mandela from prison. Mandela advocated building a South Africa in which all ethnic groups could live and work together. He persuaded the white minority that it need not be afraid of black majority rule. He also managed to calm hostility between the Zulu people and the ANC, which had led to a large amount of bloodshed.

In April 1994, peaceful democratic elections were conducted in South Africa. The ANC won an overwhelming victory. Mandela formed a government in which both F. W. de Klerk and the Zulu leader Chief Buthelezi took part. The slogan of the new South Africa was 'the rainbow nation', because in a rainbow all the different colours work harmoniously together.

A woman wearing the flag of the new South Africa celebrates Freedom Day.

Mandela told an interviewer that the apartheid government had 'used the different cultures to keep our people divided, but we are using them to unite our people. That is why we have come forward with the concept of a rainbow nation'. Although South Africa faces many problems, few people are pessimistic enough to think it will be the site of future genocide.

Openness and democracy

Of course, even in democratic multiracial societies, hatred and abuse between ethnic groups is going to occur. But there is little possibility of isolated incidents on the street turning into genocide if governments systematically oppose racism. In many countries, there are laws against discrimination and abuse on grounds of race. These are important signs that racism is not considered acceptable by the authorities.

Governments must do everything they can to encourage a basic respect for human rights and the rights of minorities. This is true both within their own countries and internationally. If all countries that fail to respect human rights are condemned, and the guilty parties are punished, the slide towards a danger of genocide may be avoided.

Killing continues. Guerrilla fighters in southern Sudan in 1998 walk past a village destroyed by government-supported militias.

A Jewish woman grieves for victims of the Holocaust. Have any lessons been learned?

The USA provides an example of the progress that can be made. The country may have been born from genocide committed against the Native American peoples, but it has changed. Despite the many racial tensions in American society, a genocidal attack on an ethnic minority group – for example, African Americans – is virtually inconceivable.

Probably the world cannot aspire to universal peace and love. Prejudice and hatred are too entrenched a part of human life. But a determined effort to encourage and enforce basic human rights could avoid the extremes of terror to which so many peoples in the twentieth century have been subjected.

Glossary

apartheid Literally, this means 'separateness'. Apartheid was the system of racial segregation that was operated by the white rulers of South Africa between 1949 and 1992.

Armenian A member of a Christian nation in western Asia.

Aryan According to the Nazis, the Aryans were a superior racial group, typically blue-eyed and blond-haired. They included Germans and Scandinavians.

authoritarian An authoritarian state is ruled by a small minority who demand a high level of obedience from their subjects and allow them little individual freedom.

communal violence Rioting or other violent acts in which different groups within a society – for example, Catholics and Protestants in Northern Ireland – attack one another.

Communist Communists believe that equality and social justice can be created by a revolution abolishing private property and establishing a classless society. Communist parties have ruled large parts of the world in the course of the twentieth century, and still control some countries, including China and Cuba.

concentration camps Heavily-guarded camps set up to hold prisoners captured in war or arrested without trial. The conditions of life are usually very poor, with high death rates.

conscripts Soldiers forced to enrol in the army whether they like it or not – the opposite of volunteers.

dehumanization The process by which a person or group of people is made to seem less than human, and therefore more vulnerable to being mistreated without respect for human rights.

democratic Relating to democracy, the political system under which people are governed by their elected representatives. In a democratic state, there is usually a high level of individual freedom.

deportation The removal of people to another country or land.

ethnic cleansing A term used in the former Yugoslavia for the process by which towns or villages with mixed populations of different ethnic groups were turned into places with a population belonging to a single ethnic group. This was achieved by driving out or killing people from minority ethnic groups.

ethnic group A collection of people who see themselves, or are seen by others, as belonging together because they are physically similar, use the same language, or follow the same religion.

guerrilla war War conducted by lightly-armed forces who avoid full-scale battle.

Holocaust The mass murder of the Jews by the Nazis between 1941 and 1945.

humanitarian Believing in the value of all human beings and the importance of helping fellow humans in distress.

hunter-gatherers Peoples who do not plant crops or have farm animals, but live by hunting game and collecting fruits and other plants that grow wild.

intervention Interference by one state in the affairs of another state.

militias Military forces made up of civilians, which support the regular army.

multicultural society A society in which the cultures of different racial or ethnic groups are allowed to flourish side by side.

multiracial society A society containing a mix of different racial or ethnic groups.

Muslim A believer in Islam, the religion founded by the prophet Muhammad in the seventh century AD.

national sovereignty The right of an independent state to control what happens within its own borders.

Nazis Members of the National Socialist German Workers' Party which ruled Germany from 1933 to 1945.

Orthodox Christians Christians in Greece, Russia, Serbia and other areas of Eastern Europe who have beliefs that differ from those of the Catholic or Protestant Churches of the West.

paramilitaries Armed groups that do not belong to an official army but often imitate military forms of organization, with uniforms, ranks and discipline.

propaganda The deliberate use of newspapers, television and other media to influence opinion or promote a cause, often employing lies and distortion.

race A group of people descended from the same ancestors, who are recognizable by physical characteristics such as the colour of their skin, eyes or hair.

racism Racism is fundamentally the belief that races are inherently different in their abilities and moral qualities, and that these differences make some races naturally superior to others. Racism is also the word used for abuse or physical attacks on people of other races based on a sense of racial superiority.

sanctions Military or economic actions taken by one state against another, to try to influence its actions or make it obey international law.

Slavs Members of an ethnic group including the Russians, Ukrainians, Poles, Czechs, Slovaks, Serbs, Croats, and Bulgarians.

tribunal A court of justice, especially one set up to enquire into one specific issue.

Books to read

Bury My Heart at Wounded Knee by Dee Brown
(Vintage, 1991)

Eichmann in Jerusalem by Hannah Arendt
(Penguin, 1994)

If This Is a Man by Primo Levi (Abacus, 1993)

Schindler's Ark by Thomas Keneally (Hodder
and Stoughton, 1982)

Srebrenica by Jan Willem Honig and Norbert
Both (Penguin, 1996)

The Gulag Archipelago by Alexander
Solzhenitsyn (Harvill, 1995)

Sources

Axis Rule in Occupied Europe by Raphael
Lemkin (Carnegie Endowment for
International Peace, 1944)

Cambodia Year Zero by François Ponchaud
(Penguin, 1978)

*Contemporary Genocides: Causes, Cases,
Consequences*, edited by Albert J. Jongman
(PIOOM, 1996)

*Genocide: Its Political Use in the Twentieth
Century* by Leo Kuper (Penguin, 1981)

Genocide Watch, edited by Helen Fein (Yale
University Press, 1992)

Guns, Germs and Steel by Jared Diamond
(Random House, 1997)

Hitler's Willing Executioners by Daniel
Goldhagen (Abacus, 1997)

The African Experience by Roland Oliver
(Pimlico, 1993)

The Fatal Shore by Robert Hughes (Collins
Harvill, 1987)

The Holocaust by Martin Gilbert (Fontana,
1989)

The Rwanda Crisis by Gerard Prunier (Hurst,
1997)

Amnesty International

Amnesty International UK, 99-119 Rosebery Avenue, London EC1R 4RE
Internet address: http://www.amnesty.org.uk/

Amnesty International has over 1 million members and supporters in some 150 countries throughout the world who contribute to its work. Members work within a closely defined mandate:

- To seek the release of prisoners of conscience – those imprisoned solely for their beliefs, colour, sex, ethnic origin, language or religion who have not used or advocated the use of violence.
- To work for fair and prompt trials for all political prisoners.
- To oppose the death penalty, torture, and other cruel, inhuman or degrading treatment or punishment of all prisoners.
- To end extrajudicial executions and 'disappearances'.

Amnesty International also works:

- Against abuses by opposition groups, such as hostage-taking; torture and killing of prisoners and other arbitrary killings.
- For asylum seekers who are at risk of being returned to a country where they might be held as prisoners of conscience, 'disappear', or suffer torture or execution.
- For people who are forced to leave their country because of the peaceful expression of their beliefs, or because of their ethnic origin, sex, colour or language.

**Amnesty International
Youth Action Network**

Youth Action is the youth movement of Amnesty International, made up of around 10,000 young people. The majority are involved in one of Amnesty's Youth Action Groups. They receive action magazines and newsletters and are involved in campaign activities including human rights concerts, letter writing, street art and cafe-crawls.

You can contact Amnesty Youth Action at the main address or e-mail: student@amnesty.org.uk

Other addresses

Center for Holocaust Studies, 1609 Ave J. Brooklyn, NY 11230, USA

Institute for the Study of Genocide, John Jay College of Criminal Justice, 444 West 56th Street, New York, NY 10019, USA

International Alert, 1 Glyn Street, London SE11 5HT

International Committee of the Red Cross and Red Crescent Societies, 17 Chemin des Crets, PO Box 372, CH 1202, Geneva, Switzerland

Index

Numbers in **bold** refer
to illustrations.